D0793461

JOHN CENA

BY MATT SCHEFF

PRO WRESTLING
SUPERSTARS

Published by ABDO Publishing Company, PO Box 398166, Minneapolis, MN 55439. Copyright © 2014 by Abdo Consulting Group, Inc. International copyrights reserved in all countries. No part of this book may be reproduced in any form without written permission from the publisher. SportsZone™ is a trademark and logo of ABDO Publishing Company.

Printed in the United States of America,
North Mankato, Minnesota
102013
012014

 THIS BOOK CONTAINS AT LEAST 10% RECYCLED MATERIALS.

Editor: Chrös McDougall
Series Designer: Jake Nordby

Photo Credits: Rick Scuteri/AP Images, cover, cover (background, 1, 1 (background), 22, 29 (inset); Marc Serota/AP Images, 4-5, 31; Matt Roberts/ Zuma Press/Icon SMI, 6-7, 20-21; Seth Poppel/Yearbook Library, 6 (inset); Carrie Devorah/WENN Photos/Newscom, 8-9, 12; Mike Lano Photojournalism, 8 (inset), 30 (top); SI1 WENN Photos/Newscom, 10-11, 28-29; Zuma Press/ Icon SMI, 13, 16-17, 18-19; Sebastian Kahnert/dpa/picture-alliance/Newscom, 14-15; Hall/Pena, PacificCoastNews/Newscom, 23; Mel Evans/AP Images, 24-25, 30 (middle); Jim R. Bounds/AP Images for WWE, 26-27, 30 (bottom)

Library of Congress Control Number: 2013945676

Cataloging-in-Publication Data

Scheff, Matt.
John Cena / Matt Scheff.
   p. cm. -- (Pro wrestling superstars)
Includes index.
ISBN 978-1-62403-134-2
1. Cena, John--Juvenile literature. 2. Wrestlers--United States--Biography--
Juvenile literature.   1. Title.
796.812092--dc23

[B]

2013945676

CONTENTS

John Cena launches an air attack against the Rock at WrestleMania.

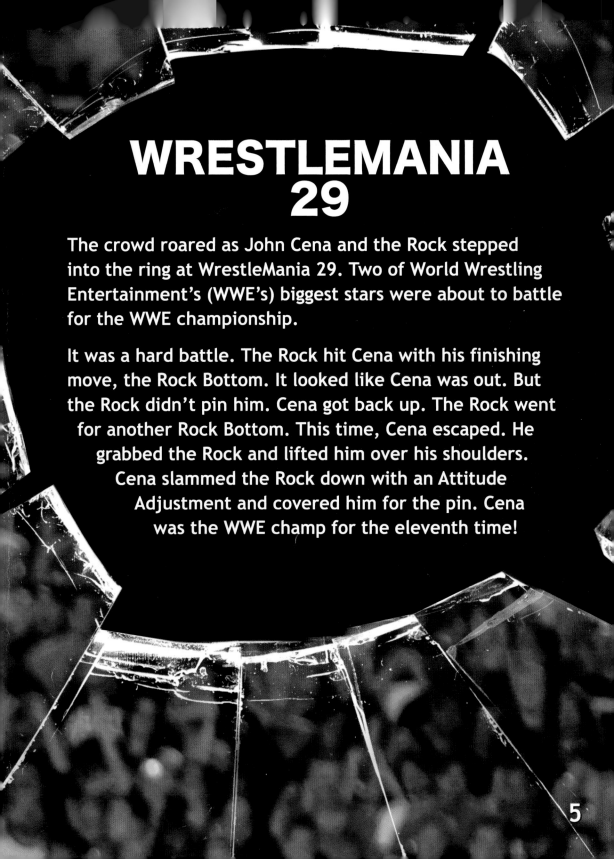

WRESTLEMANIA 29

The crowd roared as John Cena and the Rock stepped into the ring at WrestleMania 29. Two of World Wrestling Entertainment's (WWE's) biggest stars were about to battle for the WWE championship.

It was a hard battle. The Rock hit Cena with his finishing move, the Rock Bottom. It looked like Cena was out. But the Rock didn't pin him. Cena got back up. The Rock went for another Rock Bottom. This time, Cena escaped. He grabbed the Rock and lifted him over his shoulders. Cena slammed the Rock down with an Attitude Adjustment and covered him for the pin. Cena was the WWE champ for the eleventh time!

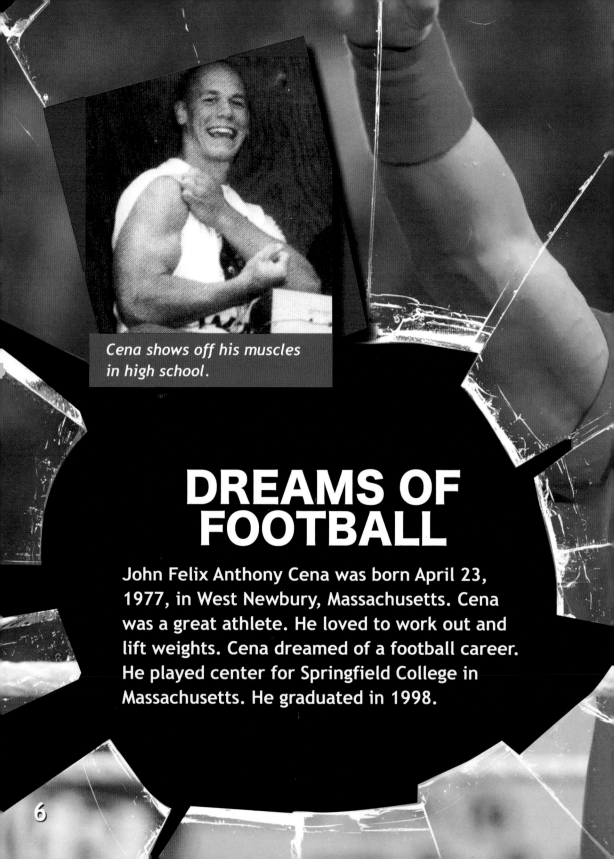

Cena shows off his muscles in high school.

DREAMS OF FOOTBALL

John Felix Anthony Cena was born April 23, 1977, in West Newbury, Massachusetts. Cena was a great athlete. He loved to work out and lift weights. Cena dreamed of a football career. He played center for Springfield College in Massachusetts. He graduated in 1998.

Few expected Cena to become a wrestling superstar growing up.

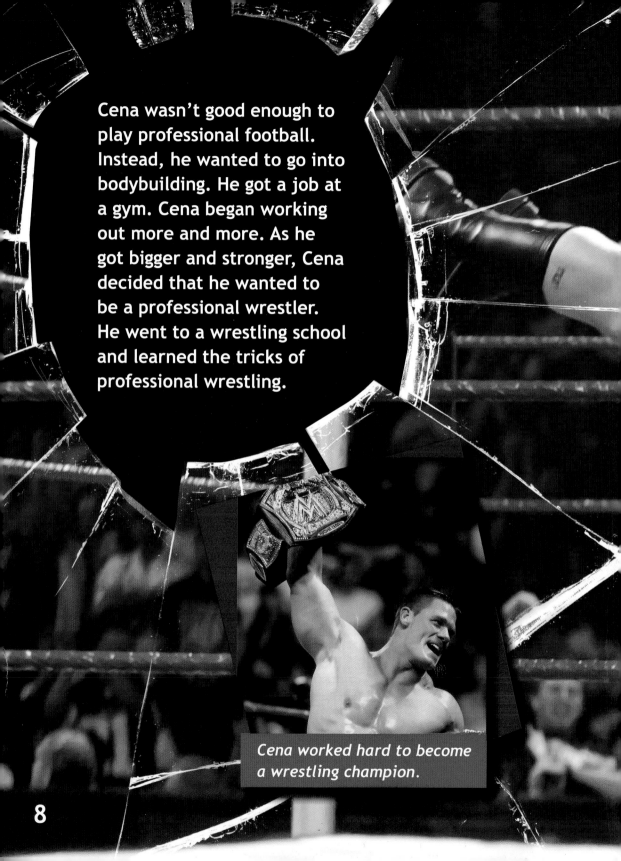

Cena wasn't good enough to play professional football. Instead, he wanted to go into bodybuilding. He got a job at a gym. Cena began working out more and more. As he got bigger and stronger, Cena decided that he wanted to be a professional wrestler. He went to a wrestling school and learned the tricks of professional wrestling.

Cena worked hard to become a wrestling champion.

Cena lifts the Big Show during a 2009 match.

FAST FACT

Cena also had a job as a limousine driver.

Cena's wrestling career started in 2000 in a small league called Ultimate Pro Wrestling (UPW). He called himself the Prototype. He pretended to be half man and half machine. Fans loved it. The Prototype dominated UPW. In April of 2000, he won the UPW heavyweight title.

Cena calls out an opponent in 2011.

Cena prepares to drop
Chris Jericho in 2005.

Cena battles John "Bradshaw" Layfield.

RISING STAR

WWE signed Cena to a developmental contract in 2001. He was sent to Ohio Valley Wrestling (OVW) to hone his skills. The Prototype continued to dominate. He won the OVW heavyweight title and also shared the tag-team title with partner Rico Constantino. He had proved he was ready for the big time. It was on to WWE!

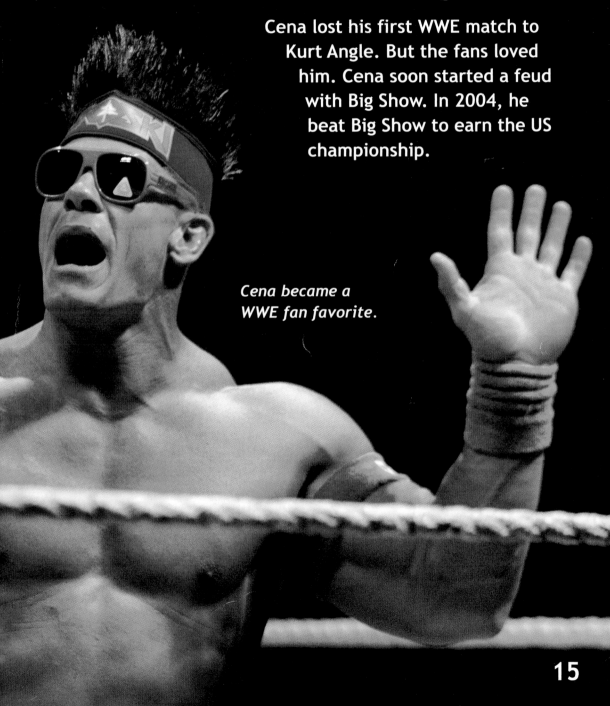

Cena began his WWE career in 2002. He pretended to be a rapper and wrestled under his own name. He gave himself the nickname the Doctor of Thuganomics.

Cena lost his first WWE match to Kurt Angle. But the fans loved him. Cena soon started a feud with Big Show. In 2004, he beat Big Show to earn the US championship.

Cena became a WWE fan favorite.

Cena tosses John "Bradshaw" Layfield at WrestleMania 21.

Cena was on the rise. He had one good finishing move, the Attitude Adjustment. But he wanted another one. So he mastered the stepover toehold facelock (STF). Cena gets his opponent face down on the mat. Then he bends the opponent's leg and pulls back on the opponent's neck. It's a powerful move from which few can escape.

Cena celebrates after beating John "Bradshaw" Layfield at WrestleMania 21 in 2005.

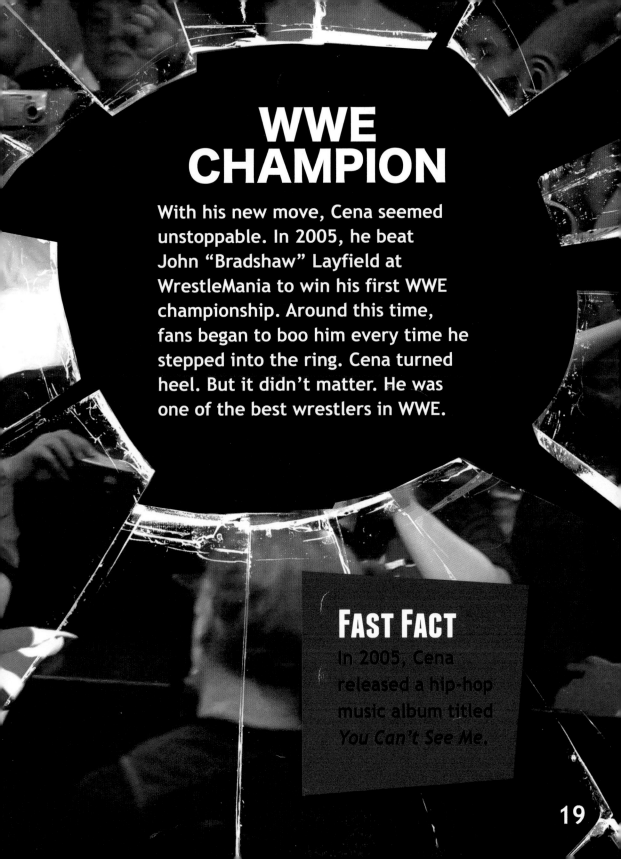

WWE CHAMPION

With his new move, Cena seemed unstoppable. In 2005, he beat John "Bradshaw" Layfield at WrestleMania to win his first WWE championship. Around this time, fans began to boo him every time he stepped into the ring. Cena turned heel. But it didn't matter. He was one of the best wrestlers in WWE.

FAST FACT

In 2005, Cena released a hip-hop music album titled *You Can't See Me.*

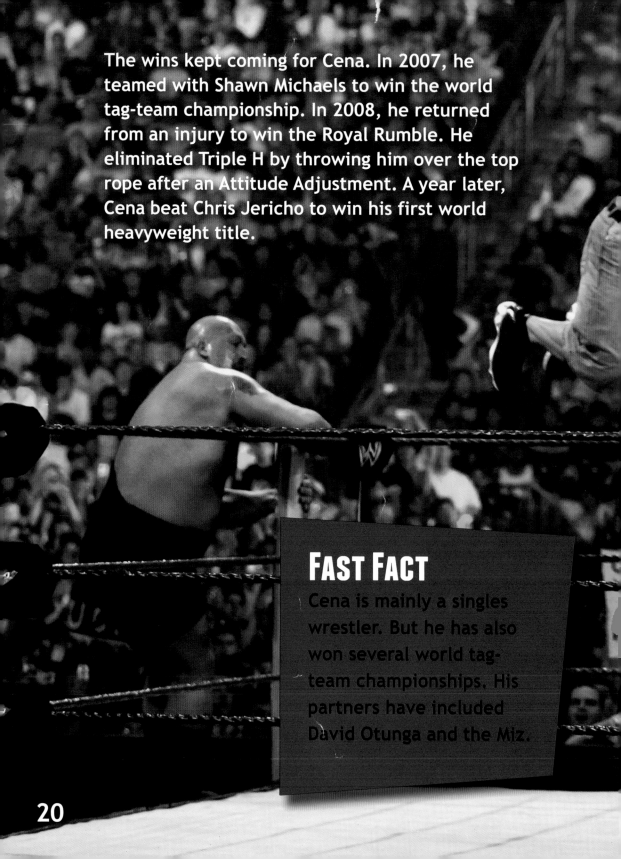

The wins kept coming for Cena. In 2007, he teamed with Shawn Michaels to win the world tag-team championship. In 2008, he returned from an injury to win the Royal Rumble. He eliminated Triple H by throwing him over the top rope after an Attitude Adjustment. A year later, Cena beat Chris Jericho to win his first world heavyweight title.

FAST FACT

Cena is mainly a singles wrestler. But he has also won several world tag-team championships. His partners have included David Otunga and the Miz.

Cena jumps from the top rope during a Triple Threat match at WrestleMania 25.

Cena rolls through Batista at WrestleMania 26 in 2010.

In 2010, Cena started a feud with Wade Barrett. But he was later forced to join Barrett's group called the Nexus. Cena refused to follow Barrett's orders and was kicked out of WWE. When he returned as a spectator, Cena attacked members of the Nexus. WWE let him return to battle his rival, and Cena beat Barrett. Then at the 2011 Royal Rumble, he eliminated almost every member of the Nexus.

Cena poses with a friend from the Make-a-Wish Foundation.

Thank you Make a wish!

FAST FACT

Cena is known for working with charities. He is active with the Make-a-Wish Foundation. He has helped grant more than 300 wishes!

Cena chokes the Rock at WrestleMania 29 in 2013.

MEGASTAR

Cena feuded with the Rock in 2011. They faced off at WrestleMania. Cena lost, but many fans described it as one of the best matches in WrestleMania history.

FAST FACT

Cena remained a constant contender for the WWE championship. From 2009 to 2013, he won the title nine times!

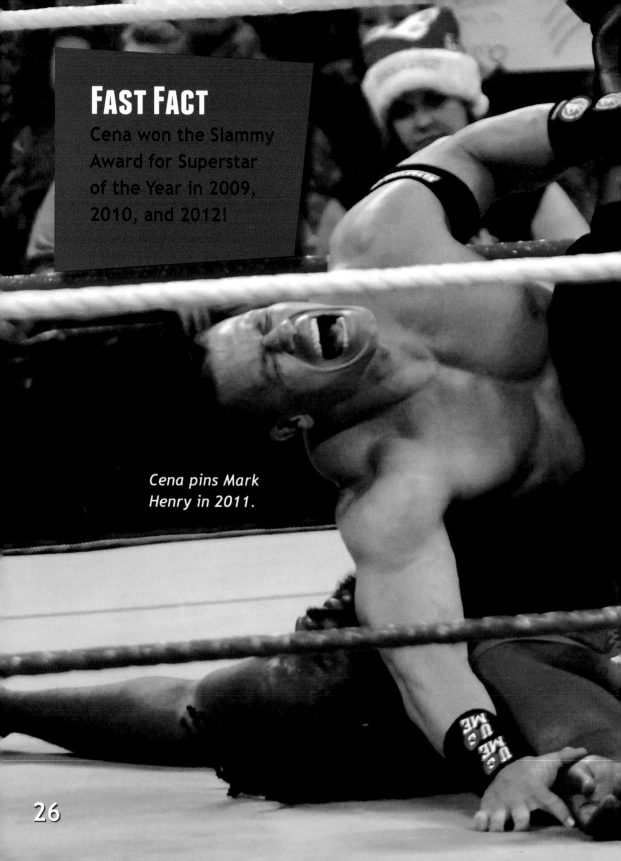

Fast Fact

Cena won the Slammy
Award for Superstar
of the Year in 2009,
2010, and 2012!

*Cena pins Mark
Henry in 2011.*

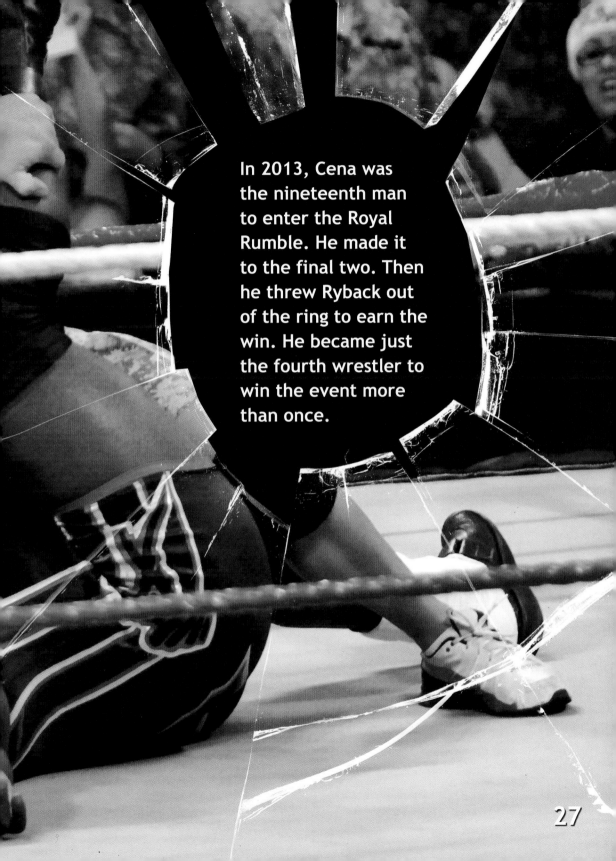

In 2013, Cena was the nineteenth man to enter the Royal Rumble. He made it to the final two. Then he threw Ryback out of the ring to earn the win. He became just the fourth wrestler to win the event more than once.

Cena is a force to be reckoned with.

Cena has also enjoyed success in his acting career. Some of his films include *12 Rounds* (2009), *Fred: The Movie* (2010), and *The Reunion* (2011). But that doesn't mean he's about to leave WWE behind. He beat the Rock at WrestleMania in April 2013 to reclaim the WWE title. He's certain to be a force in professional wrestling for years to come.

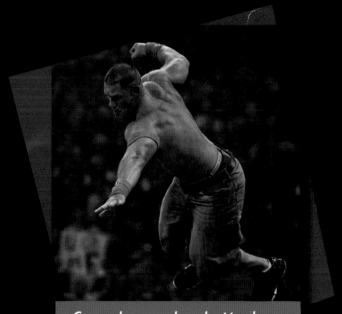

Cena drops a hard attack at WrestleMania 26.

TIMELINE

1977
John Felix Anthony Cena is born on April 23 in West Newbury, Massachusetts.

2000
Cena joins UP

2002
Cena wrestles in his first WWE match, losing to Kurt Angle.

2004
Cena beats the win the US cha.

2005
Cena releases a hip-hop music album titled *You Can't See Me*.

2006

The Marine, starring Cena, is released.

2008
Cena wins the Royal Rumble for the first time.

2013
Cena wins his seco Rumble. He also be the Rock to earn a WWE championship

GLOSSARY

bodybuilding
The act of building muscles through exercise, especially weightlifting.

charities
Organizations that provide help to those in need.

developmental contract
An agreement in which a wrestler signs with WWE but wrestles in smaller leagues to gain experience and develop skills.

feud
An intense, long-lasting conflict between wrestlers.

finishing move
A powerful move that a wrestler uses to finish off an opponent.

heel
A wrestler whom fans view as a villain.

rival
An opponent with whom a wrestler has an intense competition.

INDEX